PALMISTRY

Your Highway to Life

*Reveal your true personality and discover your
destiny in the palm of your hand*

Hazel Whitaker

PARKGATE
BOOKS

CONTENTS

CONTENTS

INTRODUCTION

PALMISTRY IS A MAP CARVED OUT IN THE PALM OF THE HAND. IT IS WITH THIS THEME IN MIND THAT YOU ARE INVITED TO TRAVEL DOWN THE HIGHWAYS AND BYWAYS OF YOUR JOURNEY INTO THE FUTURE, WHILE OBSERVING THE EXPERIENCES OF YOUR PAST.

Reading the palms of your hand is at least a fascinating study of life. At best, it is an accurate account of your past, present and future lifestyle. The more you look, the more you see. Pay attention to the detailed warning signs, and the less trouble you will bear. If you take notice of influential signs, you are less likely to miss chances for successful ventures and personal happiness.

Reading the palms is much like reading a road map. The Main Lines in your hand, i.e. the Life Line, Heart Line, and Head Line are like the main highways. The Minor Lines, i.e. Affection or Marriage Lines, Fate Line, Health Line, Travel Lines, Girdle of Venus among others, are similar to other roadways and paths, accessible to those who wish to travel them. The thumb is like a set of traffic lights indicating which route you are likely to follow. The fingers are similar to traffic signs: they signal your ability or inability to cope with your predestined journey. The Mounts of Jupiter, Saturn, Apollo, Mercury, Venus, Neptune, Mars and the Moon are not unlike well-used, reliable and favorable routes.

The absence of any or all of these mounts seems to indicate a lack of opportunity to use these particular services. Markings on the palm of the hand such as Crosses, Stars, Forks, Grids, Chains, Islands and Dots are all significant signs of good or bad fortune. They may be warning you to "proceed with caution" or signifying a safe and enjoyable crossing. Either way, these markings should be carefully studied.

Misreading the signs can lead to misconceptions, causing alarm and distress where it may not be necessary. One of the most common misconceptions in palmistry is created when a short Life Line is present. It may seem a natural assumption, because of the nature of its name "The Life Line", that if it appears to suddenly end at an early age, then so to does your life end. If you think about it logically, all the Main Lines would have to end at the same early age if this were true, plus there would have to be some sig-nificant markings on these lines, also at the same early age indicating misfortune. After all, you can't have a heart, a head, and a destiny without a life. A good palmist will look for far more detail than a short Life Line before declaring a short life span. As a student of palmistry you will do well to remember this lesson.

The purpose of this book is to introduce the novice to the art of palm reading. It is designed to be enjoyed, to be interesting as well as instructive. The reader will find the lessons simple and accurate. Palmistry has been fascinating people all over the world for very many years and students of this craft are ceaseless in their endeavors to master its accuracy. You will be amazed at your own popularity when you can take the hand of a friend or stranger and surprise them with your observations and predictions. Try to combine your new-found skills with your intuition in order to develop the psychic ability avail-able to all of us.

THE HISTORY OF PALMISTRY

Modern day palmists are well aware of the ancient history of the art of studying the palms of the hand. Palmistry dates back to the time of the ancient Hindus who are credited with its origin. Palmistry has stood the test of time as there have been many great masters of the art throughout the ages.

This fascinating "science" has never lost its universal appeal, even in today's rat race, people of all nations thirst for the secret knowledge etched out in the palms of each one of us.

"Cheiro" and Other Great Masters

"Cheiro" (Count Louis Hamon 1866-1936), a most famous and accurate palmist, devoted almost forty years of his life to the study and practice of palmistry. He traveled throughout the East, Europe and America in a tireless pursuit of perfecting his vast knowledge on the subject. His predictions were so accurate that he was consulted by many famous people. Modern day masters of the craft have benefited from his teachings, while adding their own observations and conclusions on the subject.

Casimir Stanislas D'Arpentigny was a master of palmistry who gave credence to the wealth of information portrayed by the various hand shapes which he classified into the now well-known types of Square, Elementary, Spatulate, Conic, Psychic, Philosophic and Mixed.

Adrien Adolphe Desbarrolles was a French nobleman who studied and embraced the science of palmistry with a mystical view combining it with other occult beliefs. It is believed that he gave professional consultations from his apartment in the famous, strangely named rue d'Enfer which, translated into English, means Road to Hell, though the significance of this oddity is purely coincidental.

The Gypsies

The gypsies, who are believed to have originated in India, roamed Europe through the centuries to the present day, practicing the art of palmistry. They would set up tent or even go door knocking, peddling their skills if you would "cross their palm with silver". This practice, albeit dubious, was nevertheless a popular attraction and some, though not all, were uncannily accurate. Perhaps you have heard an elderly relative say, on the telling of a story: "A gypsy told me."

Today

These days we have more educated and sophisticated means of transferring this knowledge to the enquirer or student of the craft. History has shown that palmistry does not require the student to employ psychic intuition in order to accurately predict the future or personality traits. However, modern palmists who have become psychically evolved may suggest that, given the facts learned through the masters of ancient palmistry, deeper and further information can be gleaned by employing the skills of palmistry.

But the beginner is eager to learn quickly a basic and accurate knowledge of the shapes, lines, mounts and markings which they will discover in the palms of their hands. Bearing this in mind, I have endeavored to make this book simple and straightforward, suitable for the newcomer to the art of palmistry. Creating a mystical, relaxing atmosphere with the aid of a soft, muted relaxing musical background, and the burning of a fragrant incense will enhance the flow of energy between the palmist and enquirer allowing maximum potential for an accurate and rewarding consultation.

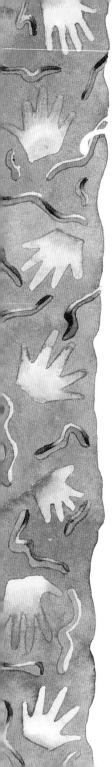

THE HANDS —
YOUR PERSONAL MAP

here are several shapes and textures of hands to be considered in palmistry, which can show at a glance some of the characteristics of the owners. The shape of the hands, fingers and thumb are important indicators of attitude and degree of dedication to that person's journey through life. From the shape of the hand alone, you can tell whether the person you are talking with is driven by logic or sentiment, whether they are pedantic or lackadaisical, whether they are creative or practical. Defining the shape of a hand is not difficult if you know what to look for and adapt a habit of observing the hands of the people you meet every day. And the "language" of the hands — the hand shake; sweaty palms; demonstrative hands — indicates behavioral patterns.

Both hands must be taken into account in palmistry. The *major* hand, which is the one used to write with, can appear to be, and often is, very different from the *minor* hand. The simple explanation of these differences is that the minor hand will show the potential you are born with, and the major hand will show if and when you reach this potential. For instance, many gifted qualities shown on the minor hand are absent or faint on the major hand. This means these talents have been unrealized for some reason. Lack of opportunity, illness or laziness can temporarily stop the flow of energy which inspires us to use our potential to its full advantage.

The "river" of life can be calm and inspiring or turbulent and destructive. The "highway" of life can be barren or fruitful. Life is a journey and palmistry can be your personal guide, mapping out the way you choose to travel.

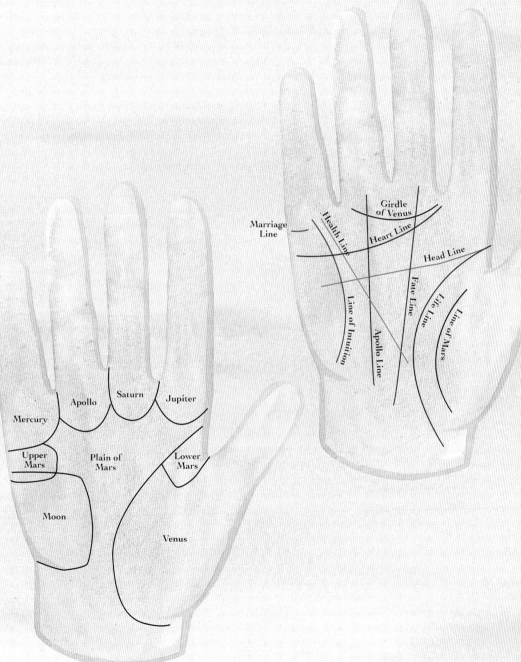

Mercury

Apollo

Saturn

Jupiter

Upper
Mars

Plain of
Mars

Lower
Mars

Moon

Venus

Marriage
Line

Health Line

Girdle
of Venus

Heart Line

Head Line

Line of Intuition

Fate Line

Life Line

Apollo Line

Line of Mars

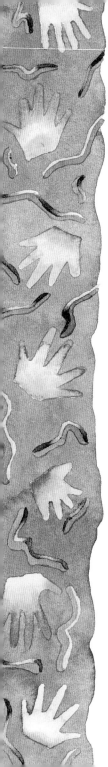

The Square Hand

A square hand is so called when the base of the fingers and the ends of the fingers are equal in width. They are the hands of a person who is down to earth, industrious and honest. What you see is what you get with these folk. They have a realistic approach to life. They are sensible and resourceful types who are well-equipped to travel the highway of life, preferring to stick by the proven roadways, infrequently using detours. Square-handed people are attracted to careers which require hard work and good business sense. It is uncommon to find weak fragmented lines on the square hand. Well-defined unblemished lines are far more common.

Unlike the other hand shapes, the position and the shape of the thumb is important on a square hand. To determine positioning of the thumb, press thumb against the Jupiter (index) finger and see at which point the top of the thumb is aligned. When the thumb is well positioned, i.e. the top comes halfway along the bottom phalange (lowest of the three sections) of the Jupiter finger and is straight, the qualities of the square hand are enhanced.

A thumb which reaches at any point below this level is considered short. This occurs when the normally principled square-handed person allows the influence of others to weaken the willpower, but when the short thumb has a bulbous or clubbed shape it becomes labeled the "elementary hand" and projects a passionate nature which sometimes lacks control. Intellectually disabled people usually have a "short-clubbed" thumb.

When the thumb is long on this hand, i.e. extending into the second (middle) phalange of the Jupiter finger, this person will combine their practical industrious qualities with strong leadership abilities.

A flexible, flat thumb, leaning backwards, is rarely found on a square hand.

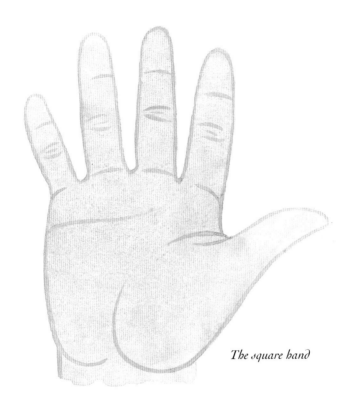

The square hand

The clubbed thumb

The flexible or flat thumb

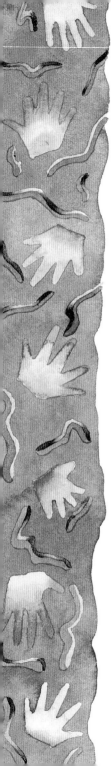

The Spatulate Hand

The spatula-shaped hand is wide at the finger tips, and narrow at the base of the hand, the wrist. It is the hand of the adventurous spirit, the explorer who loves challenge and new experiences. People with this hand shape are daring and confrontational. Rarely will they tolerate a boring journey through life because they look for adventure around every corner; for them "variety is the spice of life". They have investigative minds and are energetic and motivated.

The Conic Hand

The conic hand is sometimes called the feminine hand because it is gently rounded, and because people with this hand shape generally have sensitive, creative natures. They love the creature comforts and are optimistic. They are peace loving, family oriented and approachable. They are caring people who prefer to journey through life with a special partner. Delicate curving lines and a well-developed Mount of Venus are common to this hand, and a Head Line curving down towards the Mount of the Moon is indicative of creative abilities.

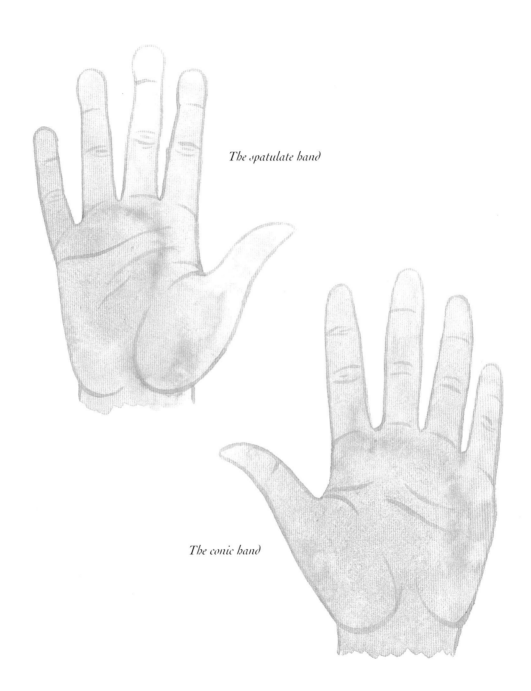

The spatulate hand

The conic hand

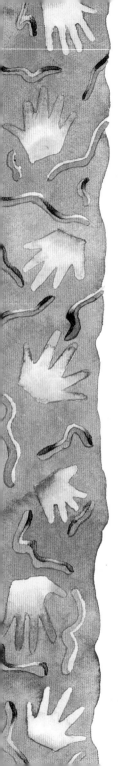

The Knotted Hand

These "intellectual" hands belong to the philosophical personality. Alert, creative, and aware of their karmic journey, these people at times become pedantic about the details of their observations. They are interesting and interested mental travelers who make good companions and teachers. Never tired of learning, people with knotted hands absorb knowledge like a sponge. They prefer a tranquil environment in which to live and work where they can escape into the realms of creativity and new ideas.

The knotted hand

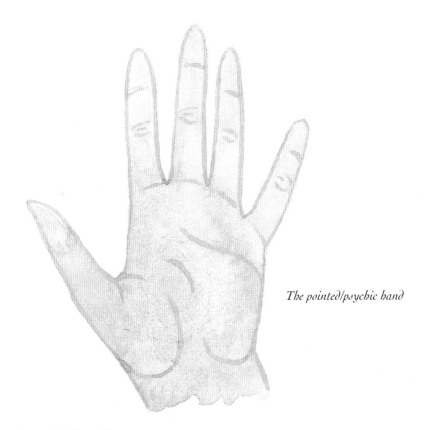

The pointed/psychic hand

The Pointed Hand

This hand shape is also known as the "psychic" hand — the fingers are delicate, long and tapered indicating sensitivity and imagination. People with pointed hands find it difficult to hide their feelings. They have sympathetic, compassionate natures, and their need for plenty of affection causes them to fall in love easily. They go through life portraying a refined and reserved attitude. Disliking confrontation, they often hide their true feelings. They are creatively gifted, with a high degree of ESP, and need to be appreciated.

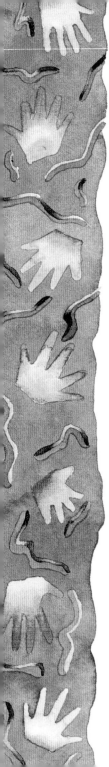

The Mixed Hand

The mixed hand may seem like an oddity and is hard to define but it is indicative of an interesting personality who views every stage in the journey of life from a different aspect.

The "mixed" hand is a mixture of two or more of the other types previously identified, and all the personality traits attributed to these types should be taken into account. For instance, a more developed radial (thumb side) of the hand signifies a personality with a strong interest in material or worldly affairs, whereas a hand which is more developed on the ulnar (little finger) side of the hand, is suggestive of a character more interested in the creative, imaginative affairs of life. Long fingers on a square palm indicate innate creative, artistic qualities governed by a practical mind. A square palm with short round fingers is indicative of a quick-witted, fast-acting personality.

Mixed hand with more developed radial side

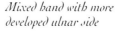

Mixed hand with more developed ulnar side

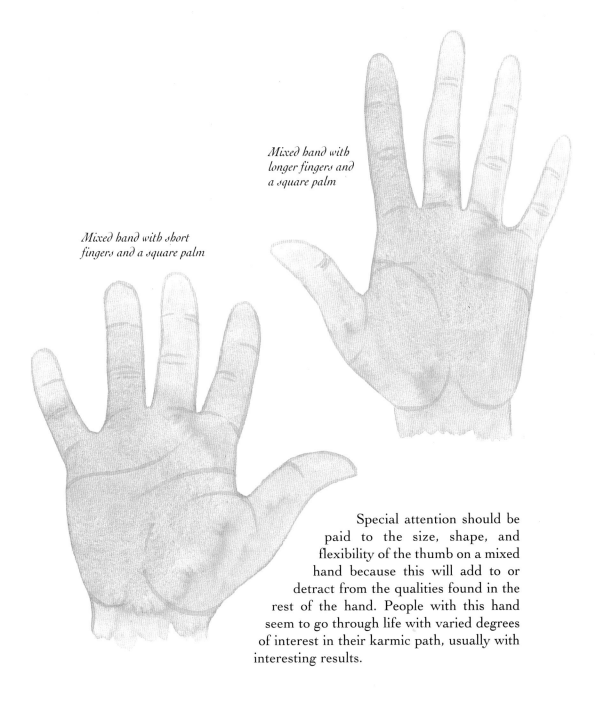

Mixed hand with longer fingers and a square palm

Mixed hand with short fingers and a square palm

Special attention should be paid to the size, shape, and flexibility of the thumb on a mixed hand because this will add to or detract from the qualities found in the rest of the hand. People with this hand seem to go through life with varied degrees of interest in their karmic path, usually with interesting results.

THE FINGERS—SIGNPOSTS

he fingers are like signposts — indicators which tell us how to use our talents and energies to their best advantage. For instance, long-fingered people are not self-motivated, but are talented and patient. Short-fingered people have initiative and are self-motivated, but they dislike repetitive work.

Each finger has the advantage of a planetary influence (opposite). The setting of the fingers on the palm of the hand varies. Fingers set in a straight line indicate an ambitious personality. A gentle curve in the formation signifies a balanced personality, and a "V"-shaped setting, an insecure nature.

Each finger is divided into 3 sections called phalanges. The top phalange represents thought, the middle phalange represents the will, and the bottom phalange represents action.

Shapes of fingers show some other personality traits:

a) Thick short fingers are indicative of an impatient rash nature. People with these fingers are focused and honest, but display little tact, and do not care for trivial pursuits.

b) Thin fingers belong to precise people with logical minds and diplomatic natures.

c) Knobby knuckles indicate a cautious, sometimes pedantic nature, especially if the top knuckles are knobbed.

d) If the middle knuckle is knotted, it signifies a personality with an orderly mind and just the right degree of logic.

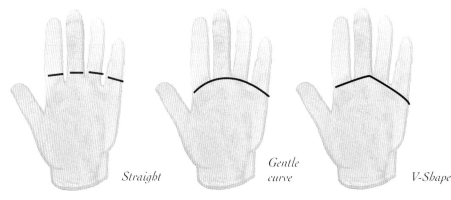

Straight

Gentle curve

V-Shape

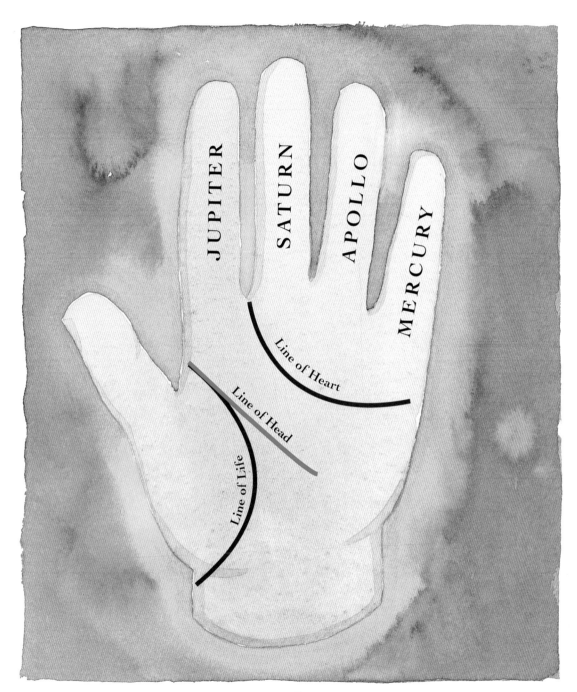

JUPITER

SATURN

APOLLO

MERCURY

Line of Heart

Line of Head

Line of Life

The Jupiter Finger

The Jupiter finger relates to originality in religion, politics, and leadership. A long Jupiter (index) finger represents a personality that is independent and strong-willed, with deeply spiritual, religious, philosophical beliefs. These people have great leadership ability and like control, often seeking power and material gain. They have well-developed egos which can, when overly fed, lead to a selfish and pompous nature. World leaders, religious hierarchy and generals are to be found with long Jupiter fingers.

Long Jupiter finger

A short Jupiter finger indicates a personality who lacks confidence. Constructive criticism tends to make these people feel inadequate. Being of a caring nature, they are open to manipulation — they need to learn to have more confidence in their own judgment.

A low set Jupiter finger indicates low self-esteem and an inclination to be extremely shy. This person has little or no courage for confrontational issues, prefers to be led rather than to lead, and has a tendency to be too eager to please.

People whose Jupiter finger is set high in the hand will stop at nothing to get their goals.

A level set Jupiter finger shows a balance of high but realistic ideals.

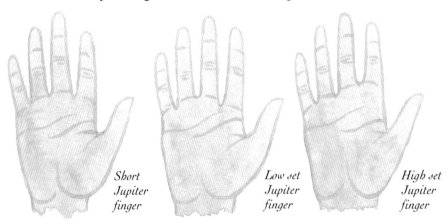

Short Jupiter finger

Low set Jupiter finger

High set Jupiter finger

The Saturn Finger

The Saturn finger is serious and down to earth. It represents the logical, practical, materialistic things in life. The person with a long Saturn (middle) finger is serious with a great ability to concentrate and absorb study; but if it is extra long, it shows a tendency towards pessimism. The Mount of Saturn (directly under this finger) should be observed for signs of temporary depression, as demonstrated by a number of fine lines. However, good organizational skills and a flair for economics are enhanced by an extra long Saturn finger. Emotional and financial security are important to these personality-types.

A short Saturn finger means this person is prepared to take challenges in business ventures, but if the Apollo finger is long, and leans towards the Saturn finger, then the challenges become risks will often lean towards gambling. Famous show business personalities tend to have the Saturn, Apollo and Jupiter fingers more or less of the same length. If the Saturn finger is only moderately short, it denotes an ability to win using intuition; but people with short Saturn fingers tend to let their winnings slip through their fingers.

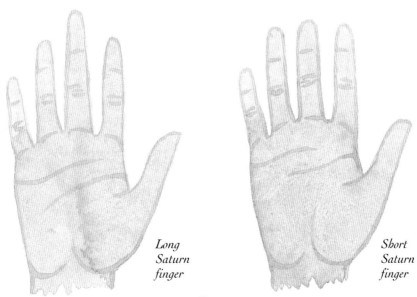

Long
Saturn
finger

Short
Saturn
finger

The Apollo Finger

The Apollo finger represents the sun — growth, expansion, luck, fame and fortune. A long Apollo finger is indicative of a family-oriented nature which likes peace and harmony. Willing and approachable, people with a long Apollo finger are energetic, sociable and creative. They are romantics who love music, the arts, and anything which adds beauty to their lives.

A short Apollo finger indicates a nature which is self-motivated and sometimes selfish. It also signifies an insecure personality who is constantly seeking reassurance. When the Apollo finger is set in line with the Saturn finger, it shows confidence and optimism, but when it is set well below the Saturn finger it shows a more practical nature.

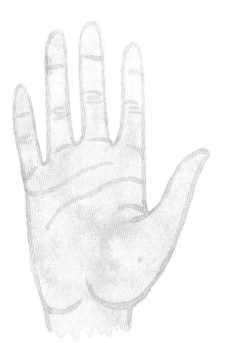

Long Apollo finger

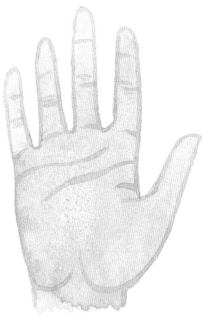

Short Apollo finger

The Mercury Finger

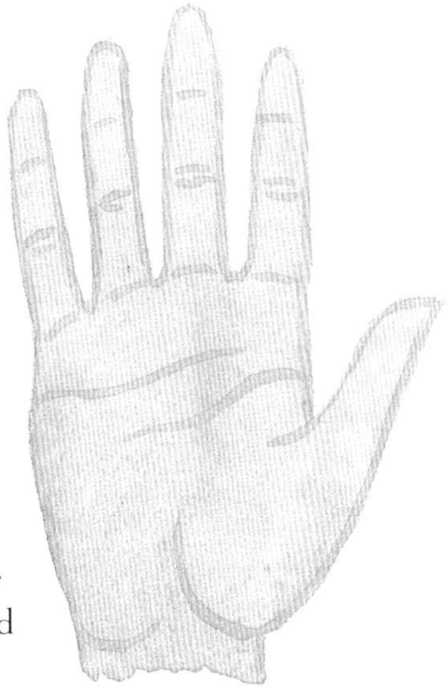

The Mercury finger represents the skills needed for communication, medicine, literature, teaching, and humanitarian activities. A long Mercury finger enforces the communication skills of the Mercury influence on this finger. It evokes curiosity in the minds of its possessor. Journalistic and creative skills are also attributed to the long Mercury finger. These personalities attract intellectual and interesting minds, and capture the imagination of an audience with their talent for public speaking and teaching. They are good negotiators and organizers.

Long Mercury finger

A short Mercury finger indicates shyness and a reserved nature lacking in confidence. In contrast to the long Mercury finger, the short version is introverted and dislikes public speaking. A very short Mercury finger often suggests a degree of problems with the libido that could require professional guidance.

When the Mercury finger is set in line with the other fingers, a confident nature is indicated. When it is set low, the owner prefers to study and practice their multitudes of talents in private.

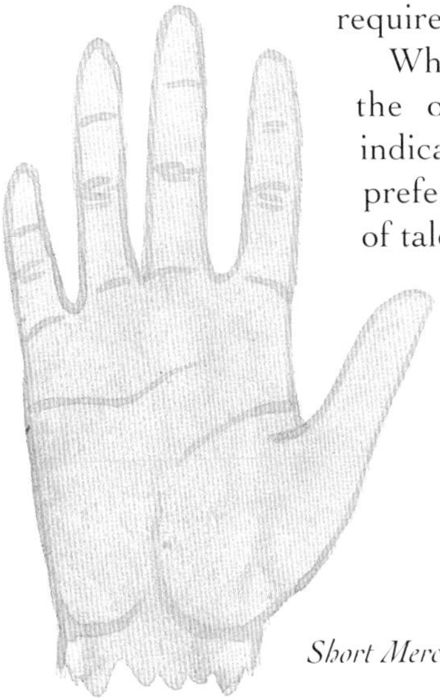

Short Mercury finger

Inclining Fingers

Sometimes the fingers are inclined to lean toward each other and special notice should be taken of the meanings. When the Jupiter and Saturn fingers are inclined, an assertive personality towards business is shown, but one with an emotionally insecure nature. Saturn and Apollo fingers inclining toward each other is associated with a personality who feels the need to satisfy family and business commitments equally. When the Mercury and Apollo fingers are inclined, a sympathetic nature is portrayed, someone who is a good listener as well as adviser.

*Inclined Jupiter
and Saturn fingers*

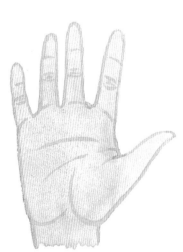

*Inclined Saturn
and Apollo fingers*

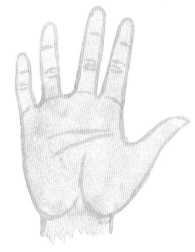

*Inclined Mercury
and Apollo fingers*

The Nails — Traffic Lights

As traffic lights prevent motorists from possible collisions, the nails warn their possessors of current or impending health and temperament problems. Of course, with modern day cosmetics, the natural color, shape and size is often disguised, but in their natural state, much information about medical conditions and personality can be gained.

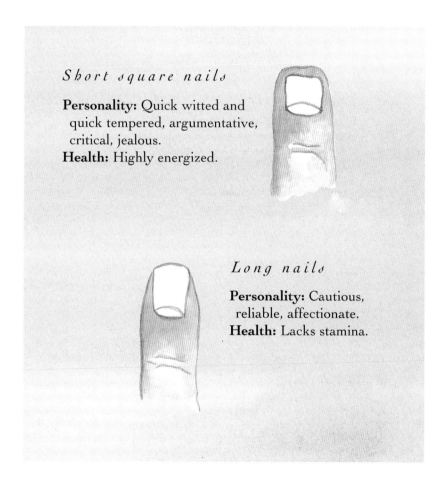

Short square nails

Personality: Quick witted and quick tempered, argumentative, critical, jealous.
Health: Highly energized.

Long nails

Personality: Cautious, reliable, affectionate.
Health: Lacks stamina.

Round nails

Personality: Good natured, kind, placid, sensitive, sensible.
Health: Indicates good energy flow. If the "moon" is very large it shows poor blood circulation.

Spatulate nails
(Shell shaped)

Personality: Moody, temperament ranges from charming and supportive to ambitious and competitive.
Health: Prone to long term illness.

Narrow nails

Personality: Ambitious, materialistic (selfish if very narrow). Can become superficial and childish when they don't get their own way.
Health: Delicate lungs.

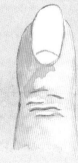

The Thumb — The Indicator

Even at a glance, the thumb is a strong indicator of personality type and business acumen. Gypsies who roam Europe have always paid special attention to shape, angle and curvature of the thumb, because valuable information can be gleaned from these and other immediate observations. Many palmists from Eastern countries take only the qualities of the thumb into consideration in palmistry. Modern palmists take the qualities of all aspects of the hand into consideration, but all of them pay special attention to the thumb.

For the first few months of a baby's life, a baby's thumb remains tucked inside its fingers. As the baby's energy and awareness grows, the hand opens and the thumb is released. When a life force is ending the thumb is often clasped inside the fingers. Also, when a person is suffering severe depression or experiencing an extreme bout of insecurity, they may be observed clutching the thumb in the palm of the hand.

When the hand is relaxed (palm up) and the thumb nail is showing side on it indicates a personality who is in control of their actions but is nevertheless easy going. When the hand is similarly positioned, but the thumb nail is sitting at the back of the hand it shows a self-disciplined personality who is both consistent and persistent, but one who has tunnel vision or is narrow-minded.

Thumb nail showing side on

Thumb nail sitting at back of the hand

The base of the thumb stems from the Mount of Venus where the energies are stored, therefore it is from the development (or under development) of this part of the thumb that physical strength and temperament can be determined. For instance, a well-developed Mount of Venus and base of thumb suggests good health and resistance to disease as well as a healthy mental capacity. These qualities are lessened when these areas are underdeveloped. The nail section or first phalange of the thumb shows the degree of willpower, and the shape of the tip of the thumb — square, conic, spatulate, round, flat or pointed (see pages 30–31) — will demonstrate the way in which the willpower will be used. When the first phalange is long, it demonstrates a strong-willed, intelligent mind. When short, its possessor is likely to use their physical energy in conjunction with their mental energy and willpower, such as athletic talent.

A square top represents a practical and sensible nature with a desire to lead.

Length

To determine the length of the thumb — long, normal, or short — refer to page 10.

A long thumb indicates leadership and organizational abilities. This person is independent, self-confident and self-reliant. In the normal position it shows a person who is well-balanced, focused, and logical. A short thumb reflects a personality who is weak-willed, easily influenced and easily distracted. A "club"-shaped short thumb is often associated with people who have a tendency towards insensitivity and aggression.

A high set thumb has an angle of about 45 degrees and indicates a personality which is a "creature of habit" who is overly cautious and emotionally restrictive.

A low set thumb has an angle of about 90 degrees and is indicative of an extroverted adventurous, enthusiastic temperament. Many famous people have a thumb which is low set.

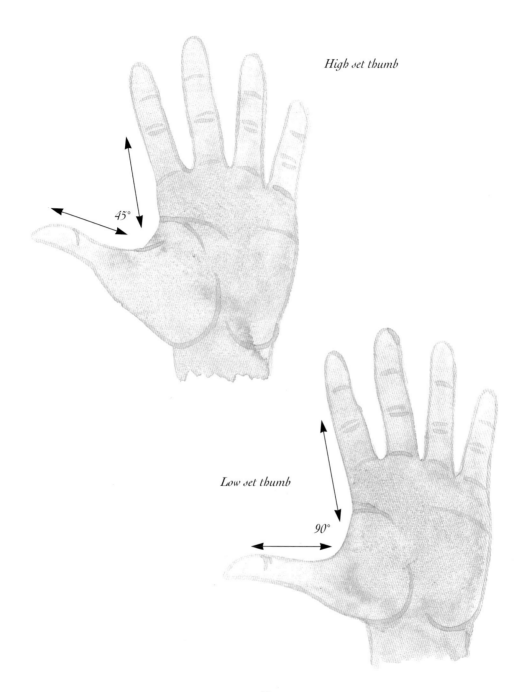

High set thumb

45°

Low set thumb

90°

Thumb Shapes

A *square top* represents a dependable personality who is well-organized and hard working — what you see is what you get.

A *conic top* represents a personality with an easy-going nature. These people are kind, gentle folk who are sometimes easily influenced.

A *spatulate top* sometimes nicknamed the "workers thumb", has acquired this label because this personality has a preference for manual crafts, putting creative skills to practical use.

A *round top* is indicative of a well-rounded personality who can balance will and authority, and is able to respect the will of others.

A *flat top* represents refinement but lacks energy — some people with this shape develop skills of manipulation through using their innate charm and power of persuasion.

A *pointed top* shows a person who needs to be needed and needs to be loved and appreciated. At times they become too eager in their desire for approval, hence making them easy targets for controlling predators.

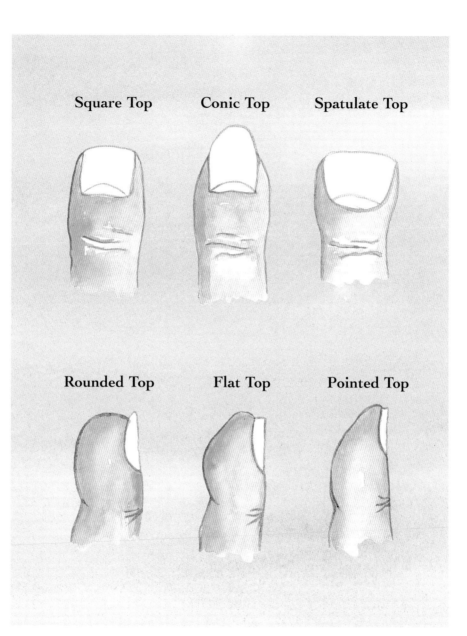

Square Top   Conic Top   Spatulate Top

Rounded Top   Flat Top   Pointed Top

THE LINES —
HIGHWAYS AND BYWAYS

iscovering the quality and quantity of your journey through life, plus knowing whether you are traveling on or off the beaten track, is valuable information which can be gained from studying the lines on the palm of your hand.

The Life, Head and Heart Lines are the most easily identifiable and are known as the Main Lines. The Fate Line is also considered by many palmists to be a Main Line, but it doesn't appear on everyone's hand. However, it is a complex line and deserves treatment equal to that of the other Main Lines. Less identifiable are the Apollo, Simian, Marriage and Children Lines, the Health Line, Girdle of Venus, Line of Intuition and Medical Line — these are known as the Minor Lines.

You will be amazed at how quickly you become familiar with the positions of the Major and Minor Lines, and how easy it then becomes to interpret the meanings of the signs which appear on them.

It is important to remember that just as the forces of nature can cause turbulence and then restore tranquillity, so too is the mind and body equipped to deal with the forces operating within and outside the body. The hand — which is after all a living organ — displays signs of trauma and good fortune, both past, present and future. By observing the warning signs nature provides for us in the palms of our hands, traumatic disturbances may be avoided, the palm later illustrating a more peaceful, healthy and rewarding experience. And by taking note of your special talents as displayed on your palm, you can explore their development to expand and enrich your life's journey.

Take your time and enjoy the illustrated lessons and the easy to follow, step by step instructions this chapter provides.

Health Line: this line will appear when there is a health problem, and disappear once health is restored.

Girdle of Venus: represents sensuality and sexuality.

Fate Line: the way we work, our partnerships, and success or failure.

Marriage Line: number and depth of serious relationships.

Head Line: the intellect, the mind, career and mental health.

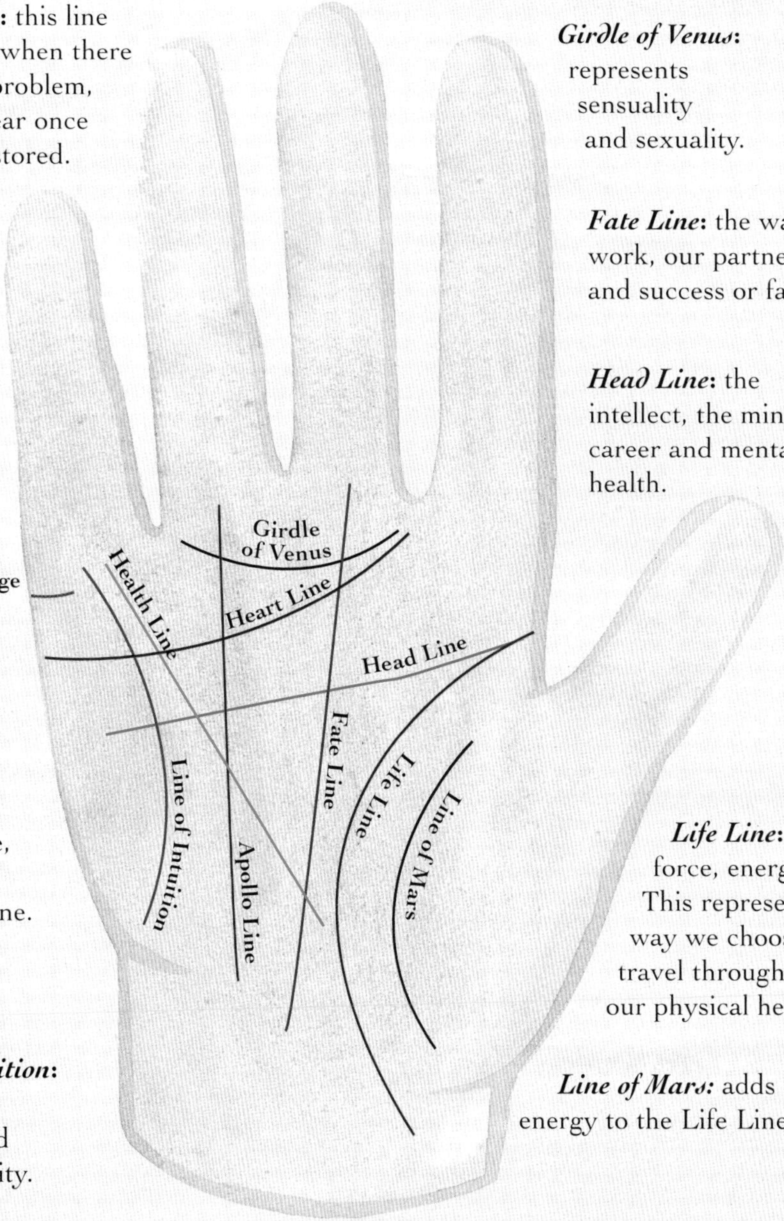

Heart Line: emotions, sensuality, and the health of the heart.

Apollo Line: home, family, creativity, the arts and fortune.

Life Line: life force, energy, drive. This represents the way we choose to travel through life and our physical health.

Line of Intuition: represents intuition and psychic ability.

Line of Mars: adds extra energy to the Life Line.

Girdle of Venus

Marriage Line

Health Line

Heart Line

Head Line

Line of Intuition

Fate Line

Apollo Line

Life Line

Line of Mars

The Life Line

The Life Line begins its journey about halfway between the base (outside edge) of the index or Jupiter finger, and the base of the thumb. It travels out and downwards toward the wrist, encircling the ball of the thumb.

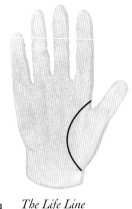

The Life Line

If Life Were Perfect...

If life were perfect, which it seldom is for any of us, you would discover a long, unbroken, well-defined line free of markings. However, you are more likely to find some problem signs. For example, if the Life Line is faint and does not have a *double* or *sister* line to support it, this would herald weakness, such as a poor energy level, or even a poor quality of lifestyle.

Faint Life Line

The Formative Years

The formative years, i.e. birth to teens, extends from the beginning of the Life Line to a point directly beneath the center of the Jupiter finger. In this section of the Life Line, you will often find the Life Line attached to the Head Line so that it appears as one. This represents the interaction of the growing mind of the child and the authoritarian influence of the parent or guardian. Often during these years, this attachment has a chained effect — this usually signifies some physical or emotional difficulties during childhood. If an island or cross appears at the very beginning of the Life Line it is indicative of some mystery surrounding the identity of the parents.

The formative years

Island or cross at beginning of the Life Line

Home or Away

When the Life Line appears to cling closely to the thumb it is indicative of a person who prefers to stay in the familiar environment of their homeland. It also signifies cautious sensitive people who lack energy and drive. When the Life Line swoops out, encircling the Mount of Venus, it is usually associated with a person who embraces the energy and adventure of life. And when a line or lines appear to cross from the Life Line into the Mount of the Moon this person will enjoy the thrill of travel.

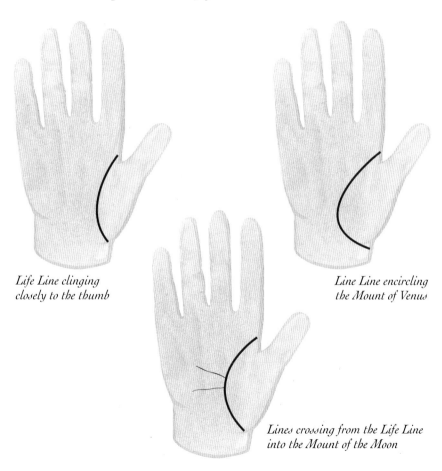

*Life Line clinging
closely to the thumb*

*Line Line encircling
the Mount of Venus*

*Lines crossing from the Life Line
into the Mount of the Moon*

Does a Break Mean Death?

A break in the Life Line does not necessarily mean life ends at that point in time. Other factors in the other lines must be taken into consideration as well as the Life Line in *both* hands. Breaks in this line do, however, indicate a sudden dramatic change of quality and standard of life, and warning signs should be heeded. Quite often the Life Line will regain its continuity a little further down the track.

Intriguing Marks

A line drooping down from the inside of the Life Line, usually indicates a loss, such as a divorce or death in the family, causing a traumatic experience. Islands, dots, breaks and crosses on the Life Line indicate temporary setbacks to the natural flow of the life force. Wherever any of these markings appear on the Life Line, attention should be paid to the meaning of that particular marking (refer to MARKINGS — SAFETY SIGNS AND WARNINGS SIGNS, pages 60–67).

Timing

For a guide to approximate timings on the Life Line, refer to diagram on page 69.

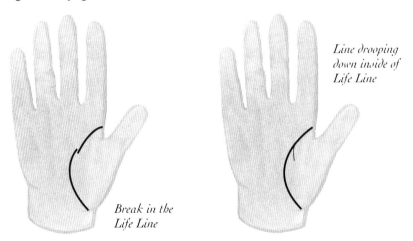

Line drooping down inside of Life Line

Break in the Life Line

The Head Line

The Head Line begins its journey at or about the same point as the Life Line. It travels across the palm towards the outer edge and when this line is well-developed, long and straight it indicates a practical mind and success in business — this is a sign of the clear, level-minded thinking of a hard-working person.

A short but well-defined line denotes the power of concentration and determined ambition.

A faint or fragile looking line, whether it be short or long, tends to be associated with a mind which is easily distracted and which becomes bored with long periods of study.

A sloping line extending to a point beneath the Apollo finger indicates a mind which enjoys the stimulation of a variety of studies and interests. If it slopes to a point beneath the Mercury finger, a creative intuitive mentality is suggested which enjoys communication, art and musical skills.

Well-developed Head Line

Short, well-defined Head Line

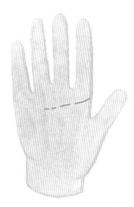

Head Line sloping to point beneath the Apollo finger

Head Line sloping to point beneath the Mercury finger

Faint Head Line

If the Head Line slopes down deep inside the Mount of the Moon, it suggests a super sensitive nature, moodiness, fears and phobic behavior, which can lead to depression. When this line tilts upwards at the end it means success in business.

Branches turning upwards at intervals on the Head Line are indicative of concentrated bursts of mental effort at the time they appear. Branches swooping downwards from the Head Line show periods of mental fatigue and stress, but these "branches" should not be mistaken for a "forked" appearance which suggests excellent literary skills. A fork at the end of a long Head Line is associated with a person who will have a longer than average working life filled with many outside interests.

Head Line sloping down deep inside the Mount of the Moon

Head Line tilting upwards at the end

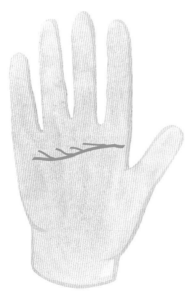

Branches turning upwards on the Head Line

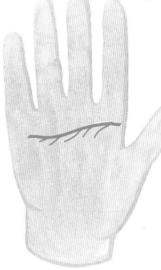

Branches turning downwards at intervals on the Head Line

If the Head Line has a "tasseled" appearance, it is a sign of worry.

A double Head Line requires special attention because it is indicative of a multi-talented person who is capable of achieving success in more than one career choice, but who has little time left for personal relationships. This person will therefore be a difficult personality to relate to or hold on to. They are likely to pursue a career which demands practical business acumen at the same time as they are pursuing a career as a professional artistic performer or sportsperson.

Islands — breaks — dots — crosses on the Head Line will appear at a time of setbacks, illness, or accidents. Refer to MARKINGS — SAFETY SIGNS AND WARNINGS SIGNS, pages 60–67.

For an idea of approximate timing on the Head Line, refer to diagram on Page 69.

Fork at the end of a long Head Line

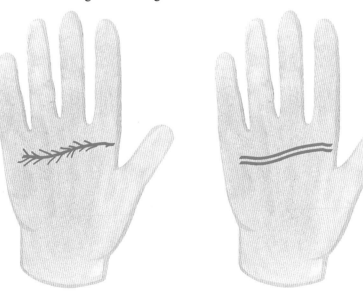

Tassled Head Line

Double Head Line

The Heart Line

The Heart Line, whether it be curved or straight, begins from a point somewhere between the Jupiter (index) finger, and the Saturn (second) finger, and travels across the palm to a point beneath the Mercury (little) finger. It represents the emotional side of the nature as well as giving information about certain areas of health. Such information is stored in the section of the Heart Line below the base of the Mercury finger, and refers to the health conditions of the heart and lungs.

When this line begins under the Jupiter finger it suggests a sensuous and spiritual affection, and indicates a person who makes a lot of demands on their partner.

Starting from beneath the Saturn finger it shows a nature which is sentimental, affectionate and placid. It represents a person who needs romance to stir their sensuous passionate side. A straight Heart Line is often associated with a person who is emotionally controlled, especially if the Head Line is more clearly defined than the Heart Line.

The more curved the Heart Line appears to be, the more emotional and sensual the possessor is. People with curved lines are not afraid to openly demonstrate their emotions, nor are they afraid to express their disappointments in love when a relationship ends.

The Heart Line

Heart Line beginning
under the Jupiter finger

Heart Line beginning
under the Saturn finger

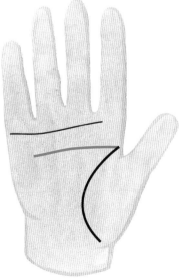

Straight Heart Line

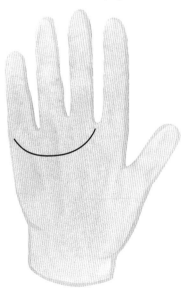

Curved Heart Line

Branches leading downwards from the Heart Line show a person cautious in forming relationships for fear of rejection, probably due to a past traumatic experience.

There is such a thing, known as a Semi-Simian Line, which need special consideration. The difference between this unusual formation and the Simian Line, is that the Semi-Simian Line has the appearance of the Heart and Head Lines having their own beginnings, but joining up together to give the *appearance* of one line, while the Simian Line is one very well-defined line right across the hand. People with this line seem to have some confusion about their sexuality, but this does not necessarily mean they are homosexual. The confusion may be the result of other phobias and fears, i.e. they may be more involved with their careers or some sporting activity, but wherever they decide to direct these energies, sexual gratification will not have top priority.

Branches leading downwards from the Heart Line

Short branches curving down from the Heart Line suggests short-term relationships.

Chains on the Heart Line represent traumatic relationships. Breaks represent sudden dramatic endings of relationships. Double Heart Lines are indicative of a person who is a loyal and devoted partner

For further explanations, see MARKINGS — SAFETY SIGNS AND WARNING SIGNS, pages 60–61). For an approximate idea of timing on the Fate Line, refer to diagram on Page 69.

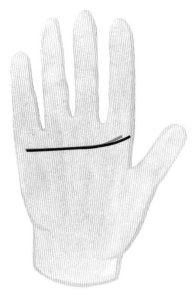

Semi-Simian Line

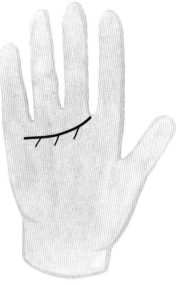

*Short branches curving
down from the Heart Line*

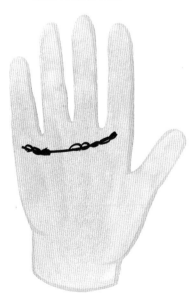

Chains on the Heart Line

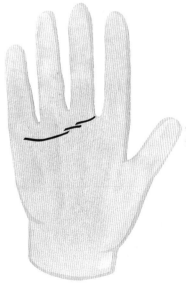

Breaks in the Heart Line

The Fate Line

The Line of Fate begins its journey at the wrist and travels up the palm towards the Saturn finger. When it appears apart from the Life Line it signifies independence at an early age and foretells a person's desire to "leave the nest" early. The bigger the gap between the Head and Fate Line, the bigger the gap between the subject and their parents, both geographically and physically.

However, if there are faint lines connecting the Fate Line to the Life Line it indicates the subject will retain a good relationship with their parents, albeit from a distance.

If the Fate Line begins its journey as part of the Life Line, it suggests the subject will be strongly influenced by their parents' guidance and support early in their career, sometimes resulting in the subject becoming part of a family business venture. But this by no means suggests a dependency or "sponging" because the very existence of the Fate Line is evidence of a person's sense of responsibility.

However, when the Fate Line begins *inside* the Life Line, it does indicate the subject could allow their family to persuade them towards a choice of career as well as influence decisions over personal matters.

Particular notice should be paid to lines running into and joining the Fate Line. These are called Attachment Lines because they indicate

The Fate Line

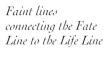

Faint lines connecting the Fate Line to the Life Line

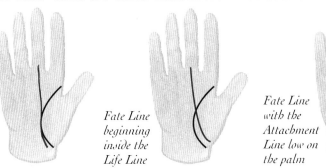

Fate Line beginning as the Life Line

Fate Line beginning inside the Life Line

Fate Line with the Attachment Line low on the palm

marriage relationships. When such a line joins the Fate Line low on the palm, it indicates that the subject is willing and able to take responsibility of such a commitment early in life.

If the Attachment Line is long before joining the Fate Line, it means there will be a long union before the marriage. If the Attachment Line stems from the direction of the Mount of Venus it suggests the union was work related or introduced through a member of the family circle.

Long Attachment Line

If the Attachment Line stems from the direction of the Mount of the Moon it indicates the union was instigated by influences outside the family environment, and may be from another state or country.

The absence of these Attachment Lines does not mean there is absence of committed relationships; but it does suggest the subject may not be ready for marriage at the time of commitment, often resulting in problems which show up in other parts of the palm.

Career changes are indicated by a forked or "Y"-shaped split in the Fate Line.

Crosses, stars, breaks or islands which appear on the Fate Line are indicative of setbacks to the subject's goals and ambitions (see MARKINGS — SAFETY SIGNS AND WARNING SIGNS, pages 60–61). For an approximate idea of timing on the Fate Line, refer to diagram on Page 69

Attachment Line pointing away from the Mount of Venus

Attachment Line pointing away from the Mount of Venus

Forked or "Y"-shaped split in the Fate Line

The Minor Lines

While the Main Lines are easy to identify, the Minor Lines very often show a slight difference in place and direction from palm to palm. For a demonstration of how these lines might look on a living palm, see illustrations in EXAMPLE DESTINIES on pages 71 and 75.

The Apollo Line

The Apollo Line, when it is present, heralds a fortunate life for its subject. In its entirety, it travels from within the Mount of the Moon at the wrist to a point beneath the Apollo finger. However, since the journey of life is seldom completely free of difficulties, the Apollo Line more often appears at irregular intervals, and in many hands is difficult to distinguish.

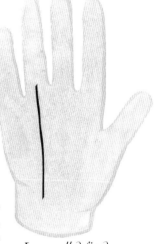

Long, well-defined Apollo Line

Whether the subject decides to use fortunate circumstances of birth, their innate creative talents, or the advantages of a union with another person so blessed, will be demonstrated by the appearance and condition of this line, e.g. a well-defined long Apollo Line shows an uninterrupted successful journey.

A line beginning between the Head and Heart Lines with a faint appearance and ending in a fork, indicates a career which loses prestige and financial benefit. When the Apollo Line is well defined but starts late, it suggests good fortune resulting from a late starter, someone who "missed the bus" early in life but made up ground after applying determination and effort.

Faint Apollo Line ending in a fork

The absence of this line is not an indication of bad luck or no success, it is more than likely just a sign of lack of interest in achieving success.

Frayed lines, islands and crosses represent periods of setbacks because of illness or temporary failure (see Markings — Safety Signs and Warning Signs, pages 60–61). For an approximate idea of timing on the Apollo Line see Timing — When Will I Arrive? pages 68-69.

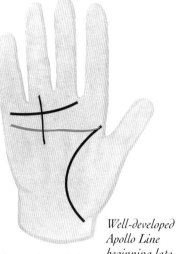

Well-developed Apollo Line beginning late

The Simian Line

This unusual sign appears as a straight line across the palm of the hand, seemingly combining the Head Line and the Heart Line as one entity. Modern palmists are reluctant to label this peculiar formation as the Simian Line which suggests an ape or monkey-type palm.

The peculiar personality traits associated with this line are related to the confusion of its possessor in determining a priority between affairs of the heart and emotions, and the practical, logical mentality shown by a straight line. These people seem to have difficulty separating intellect and emotion, or concentrating on both of these instincts at the same time.

The Simian Line

My personal advice to people with this line, regarding relationships, is to settle for nothing less in a partner than one who can offer an equal amount of intellectual and emotional support, because they find it hard to cope with an uneven balance.

It is difficult to interpret markings on this line, since it is not always possible to tell whether the signs are reflecting an intellectual or emotional problem — this leads to even more confusion (see Markings — Safety Signs and Warning Signs, pages 60–61). For an approximate idea of timing on the Simian Line, refer to diagram on Page 69

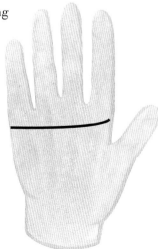

The Marriage Lines

Perhaps because palmistry is such an ancient art, some of the traditional lifestyles and values inspired students of the craft to label some of the lines appropriately. The Lines of Marriage are a typical example of this. Modern palmists are more inclined to refer to these lines as Affection Lines, because in today's world, long-term serious relationships do not always result in a commitment to marriage. It is therefore advisable to use the Attachment Line on the Fate Line as a cross reference in these matters.

The Marriage Lines are situated on the outside edge of the palm between the base of the Mercury (little) finger and the Heart Line. Well-defined lines are representative of the relationships which result in long-term commitments, and faint lines represent relationships which are significant but passing influences.

For an approximate idea of timing, measure the distance between the base of the Mercury finger and the Heart Line. The halfway mark should represent the age of 25 years or thereabouts.

Will it last?
Straight well-defined Marriage Lines without markings indicate a lasting commitment. A Marriage Line ending in a "fork" suggests a sudden ending of the marriage. Many forks on the Marriage Line are associated with a person's persistence in trying to make a difficult marriage work. A Marriage Line which curves up towards the Mercury finger suggests the marriage partner's improved success during the relationship. If the line curves downwards, touching or passing through the Heart Line, it foretells a dramatic ending to the marriage, the result of the partner's destiny taking a sudden change of direction.

When a forked appearance shows at the beginning of the Marriage Line (outside edge) it signifies that obstacles and difficulties will cause delays and separation before marriage.

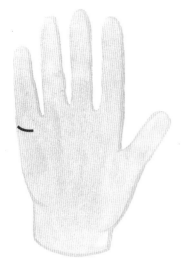

The Marriage Lines

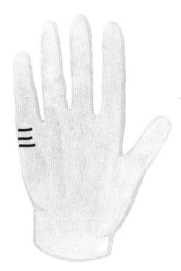

Well-defined Marriage Lines

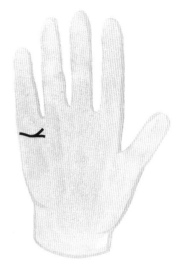

Marriage Lines forked at end

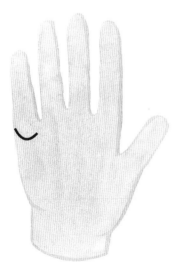

*Marriage Line curved up
towards Mercury finger*

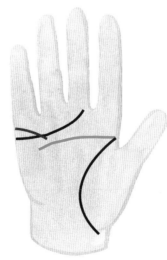

*Marriage Line passing
through the Heart Line*

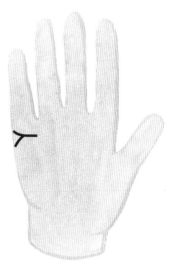

*Marriage Line forked
at beginning*

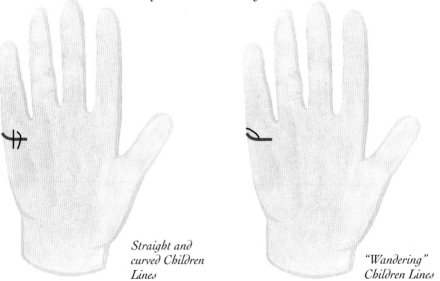

The Children Lines

Very close scrutiny is necessary in defining the Children Lines, because they can be confused by the lines of stress or worry which sometimes occupy the same space. However, on *very* close inspection, it is possible to identify the number and sex of the children.

The Children Lines are those faint lines which touch or cross the Marriage Line. Child carers have many faint lines in this area but they do not touch or cross the Marriage Line.

Straight lines indicate boys, and curved lines indicate girls.

If the Children Lines appear to "wander" away from the Marriage Line it suggests a behavioral problem in the child which causes them to want independence too early in life.

The Children Lines

Straight and curved Children Lines

"Wandering" Children Lines

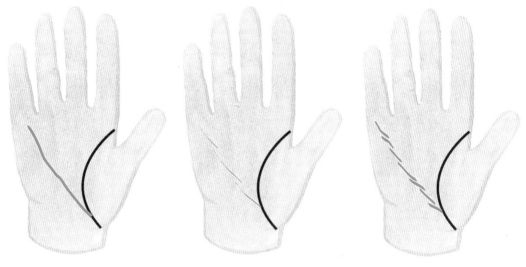

The Health Line   *Broken Health Line*   *Frayed Health Line*

The Health Line

Should you experience confusion identifying this line, please do not be alarmed, for it does indeed seem to serve a dual purpose, i.e. the Health Line appears on the palm during times of sickness, but it also appears on the palms of healers who may be either physical, mental, or spiritual practitioners. Therefore it seems to indicate that its absence on the palm means either freedom from sickness or that the subject is not involved with the healing of others.

When it is present, its natural position and formation begins near the Life Line, and travels upwards, across the palm, to a point on or beneath the Mount of Mercury.

If the Health Line appears broken or frayed it denotes periods of ill health for the subject, or periods of responsibility for the health of others, e.g. aged parents, which in turn takes a toll on the health of the carer.

The Girdle of Venus

There is always much debate between palmists on the function of the Girdle of Venus, a line which extends from between the Jupiter and Saturn fingers to between the Apollo and Mercury fingers. Some say it is an indication of sexual vigor and maturity, some maintain the belief that it is a sign of emotional sensitivity, while others are convinced that a well-defined Girdle of Venus suggests sexual aggression, especially if the Mount of Venus is also well developed. These old beliefs, however, seem to have been founded in the days of sexual repression — now we accept that a healthy sexual appetite is normal.

The fact that the Girdle of Venus rarely appears on Square or Spatulate hands (which represent practical minds) and are often found on Conic, Knotted or Pointed shapes (representing sensitive, emotional personalities) seems to verify the modern palmists opinion that the Girdle of Venus deserves its sensuous reputation. It is my conclusion, however, that the Girdle of Venus is indicative of a healthy, sensitive, sensuous nature.

A broken Girdle of Venus may suggest an overly sensitive and hysterical disposition.

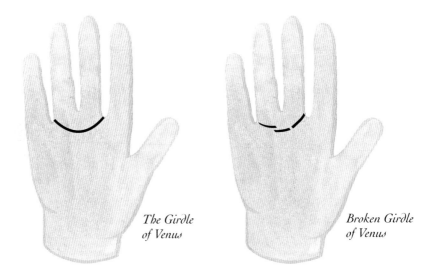

The Girdle of Venus

Broken Girdle of Venus

The Line of Intuition

The Line of Intuition begins low down on the Mount of the Moon, and curves upwards into the Mount of Mercury. A long, well-defined Line of Intuition signifies a personality who is very sensitive, and gifted with psychic ability.

When the line is faint, it has the same meaning but to a lesser degree.

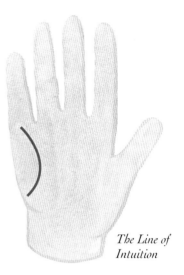

The Line of Intuition

The Medical and Teaching Lines

The Medical Lines are situated above the Heart Line and beneath the space between the Apollo and Mercury fingers. They are indicative of people with a vocational inclination towards the caring of other people, especially in the medical field.

These lines should not be confused with the line or lines beneath the Mercury finger itself, which represent teaching skills.

If the Teaching Lines connect with the Medical Lines, it indicates the subject has abilities in the area of spiritual healing and the teaching of spiritual matters.

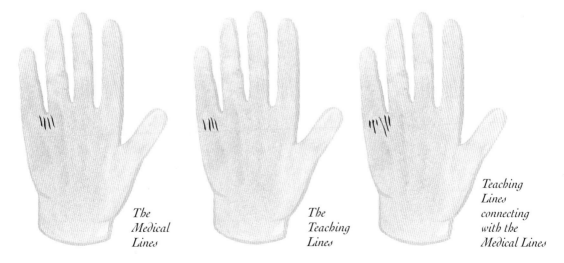

The Medical Lines

The Teaching Lines

Teaching Lines connecting with the Medical Lines

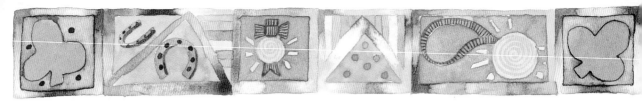

The Mounts —
Flat Land or Mountains

Situated in various parts of the palm are the Mounts. They are over- or underdeveloped sections of the palm each governed by the influence of a planet, hence entitled the Mounts of Jupiter, Saturn, Apollo, Mercury, Venus, Moon, and Upper and Lower Mounts of Mars.

The qualities of these planetary influences are enhanced in the personality when they are well developed. Under-developed Mounts simply suggest that the subject does not have the need or desire to use the benefits of those planetary influences at this point in their journey. The subject may be observed developing the use of one or more of these influences if and when it becomes advantageous to do so, for instance, a person traveling a creative path in life will not need the aggressive influence of the planet Mars in order to achieve success, whereas a military or political career would benefit from its forceful influence.

Similarly, a person pursuing a career which requires the skills of imagination, writing, teaching, and communication would benefit from the influences of the Moon and Mercury. People who change career paths regularly often show evidence of this through the well-developed Mounts of several planetary influences.

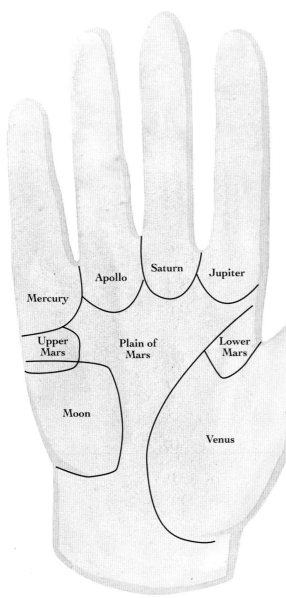

Mount of Jupiter: ambition, drive, willpower, religious beliefs, philosophies

Mount of Saturn: practical, material and scientific outlooks, dedication and responsibility

Mount of Apollo: home and family, and creativity

Mount of Mercury: communication, business acumen, honesty, literary and teaching skills

Apollo
Saturn
Jupiter
Mercury
Upper Mars
Plain of Mars
Lower Mars
Moon
Venus

Mount of Venus: the home, family, love, stamina, sensuality and values

Mount of the Moon: the imagination, intuition, travel and freedom

Mount of Upper Mars: courage, resilience and temper

Mount of Lower Mars: military skills, resistance and bravery

Mount of Jupiter

The Mount of Jupiter represents power, ambition, logic and ego and when this Mount is well developed, it suggests a personality who is using these qualities to their best advantage. It shows potential for leadership and organizational ability; strong political and religious beliefs; and an authoritarian nature. When the Mount of Jupiter is flat, the subject is unlikely to pursue these ambitions, and if this Mount has an overly-developed appearance there is possibly an inclination towards bigotry, arrogance, selfishness and bullying.

Mount of Saturn

The Mount of Saturn represents the serious attitude towards the achievement of material gain and recognition. People with scientific, investigative minds have a well-developed Mount of Saturn. They care nothing for trivial pursuits, nor do they easily tolerate people governed by their emotions. If the Mount of Saturn is overly developed it signifies a person who will become pessimistic, solitary and too cautious in their attitude to the journey of life. This is one case therefore when a flat Mount of Saturn represents a person who, although governed by logic and strong ideas, nevertheless has an approachable personality. Careers which attract these people are in medicine, science, and economics.

Mount of Apollo

The Mount of Apollo, governed by the Sun, represents creativity, family, growth, expansion and good fortune. A well-developed Mount of Apollo shows a personality which appreciates beauty, nature, creativity, the arts, children, family and animals. Special attention is given to the markings on this Mount because it can herald good luck and success plus financial gains.

When the Mount of Apollo is excessively developed, is suggests hedonistic behavior, the result of too much good fortune. An underdeveloped Mount of Apollo indicates that, for the time being, the subject's interests and expectations in these areas are not active. Famous successful people have well-developed Mounts of Apollo with distinctive markings.

Mount of Mercury

The Mount of Mercury is associated with communications, self expression, literary skills and personal relationships. A well-developed Mount of Mercury suggests an approachable, confident personality who is a good mediator. Good business, teaching and journalistic skills are also evident in a person with a well-marked and developed Mount of Mercury. When this Mount is flat or underdeveloped, it is indicative of a shy personality with poor business skills and one who has difficulty in expressing themselves. If this Mount is excessively developed, it suggests a personality who is inclined to be perceptive and a confidence trickster.

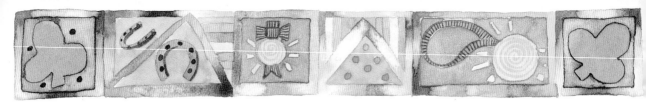

Mount of Venus

The Mount of Venus represents emotional and physical energy — love, creativity, and drive. A well-developed Mount of Venus suggests a personality who knows how to appreciate and enjoy life to the full. They are sociable beings with a taste for good food, wine, good music, and good humor. They are sensual and attracted to beautiful people. However, if this Mount is full but too soft or floppy in appearance, it may indicate a personality prone to overindulgences who is greedy for the pleasures of life.

A flat, tight Mount of Venus suggests a personality who lacks stamina, is almost uninterested in pursuing life's pleasures, and is intolerant and unsympathetic towards people who indulge themselves in the material and physical aspects of life.

Mount of the Moon

The Mount of the Moon represents imagination, creativity and travel. A well-developed Mount of the Moon indicates a personality with good creative and imaginative skills. People who are attracted to and skilled at water sports, e.g. swimming, fishing, boating, or have a naval career, have well-marked and well-developed Mounts of the Moon, as do people who love travel and those with creative imaginations. Similarly, people who dislike travel, are not creative, and do not possess a vivid imagination, will have a flat of underdeveloped Mount of the Moon.

Upper Mount of Mars

The Upper Mount of Mars represents courage as well as aggression. When this Mount is well developed it is indicative of a confrontational personality who can deal with a crisis in a practical manner. These people may be attracted to careers in the military. An underdeveloped Upper Mount of Mars suggests a personality who dislikes confrontation and is inclined to react in shock at sudden catastrophic circumstances. When these people are affected by the aggressive influences of the planet Mars, they prefer to play the role of protective aggressors.

Lower Mount of Mars

A well-developed Lower Mount of Mars is a sign of an aggressive nature. These people tend to like war games and aggressive sports. They seem to enjoy making a battle out of life's journey, attacking life rather than submitting to it. "Get life before it gets you" seems to be their motto. The apparent absence of a Lower Mount of Mars suggests that the subject has not encountered aggressive conditions for the time being, and will avoid volatile conditions.

Important Markings

Safety Signs and Warning Signs

As well as the condition and length of the Main and Minor Lines, there are a variety of markings on the palm. These appear and disappear in accordance with the coming and going of eventful periods in your life. Each of these markings has a general meaning of their own, but of equal importance is their position on the lines.

Because the Markings are warning signs, very often they will appear in time for you to heed the warning. Then they disappear. But sometimes we choose to learn through experience and flirt with danger.

The characteristics shown in the shape of your hands, the fingers, the thumb and the Mounts will indicate which choice you are likely to make.

Here are some short rhymes relating to each of the markings to help you remember their general meaning.

Crosses	Crosses on parts of the palm will appear
	Whenever a time of trouble is near
Squares	Boxes or Squares are a sign of protection
	From danger which lurks from unwanted infection
Chains	Chains which have formed upon any line
	Are indicating a difficult time
Breaks	Breaks in a line of the palm indicate
	Short setbacks of a temporary state
Dots	Small Dots appearing need special attention
	These are a sign of Fate's intervention
Triangles	Signs of a Triangle signal despair
	Do not take chances, be wise and beware
Stars	A Star on the Mount of Apollo brings money
	Sometimes on Venus, a good looking honey
Grilles	Grilles are quite simply lines in excess
	Excessive behavior leads to distress
Tassels	Lines that are tasseled mean energy drained
	When you overdo things there's nought
	to be gained
Branches or	Improvement is noted when Branches arise
Forked Lines	Drooping Branches can mean "sad surprise"
Islands	Problems and Islands are one and the same
	Did you create them? Or is Fate to Blame?

Dots

Sometimes a dot will appear on one or more of the major lines. These dots are difficult to see without the aid of a good magnifying glass, because they are usually no bigger than a pin prick. However, once you have managed to identify them, you will find they seem to be as noticeable as the "cat's eyes" on a highway. Dots are warning signs, signaling danger to a specific part of yourself as you journey through life — and, like many other warning signs in the world, they are red or, at the least, very pink in color.

On the Life Line, dots indicate a sudden acute attack on the natural flow of energy, brought about by a serious, albeit temporary, illness which occurs at the time of their presence. These dots will wither and disappear, or signify a cure by the appearance of a circle or square around them, when the energy is restored.

On the Head Line, they are indicative of a head injury or severe mental stress at the time of their appearance. They disappear when the problem has been resolved.

When on the Heart Line, in order to ascertain the source of the problem, it is necessary to divide the Heart Line into three sections A, B and C. The "A" section is the part going from between the Jupiter finger to the middle of the Saturn finger; the "B" section goes from the middle of the Saturn finger to the middle of the Apollo finger; the "C" section goes from the middle of the Apollo finger to the end of the Mercury finger. Nominate "A" to matters of the affections; "B" to matters of sensitivity; and "C" to the medical condition of the heart and lungs.

Dots appearing on the "A" section would indicate a sudden, dramatic change of affection, as in the case of a broken relationship which results in a "broken heart". A dot on the "B" section signifies a super-sensitive reaction to some unfortunate circumstance. A dot appearing on the "C" section will refer to a medical condition of the heart or lungs — if such a dot appears, you must get verification from a fully qualified medical practitioner.

On the Fate Line, dots suggest an interruption to the progress of career and success, possibly the result of the unfortunate choice of an unsupportive business partner.

On the Apollo Line, dots suggests a shock to the system, the result of adverse circumstances that temporarily stop the flow of success people with the Apollo Line invariably have.

Crosses

Crosses are formed on, above or below the major lines during periods of unexpected difficulties. They represent situations which temporarily suspend the normal course of events, and often leave the subject shaken but wiser for the experience.

On the Life Line, crosses are a sign of some physical challenge requiring determination to overcome.

On the Head Line, a cross represents a "mental block" such as that which occurs through mental exhaustion or torment.

When on the Heart Line, if a cross appears on the "A" section, it indicates a situation where the affections are thwarted. On the "B" section, it suggests emotional trauma, and when it appears on the "C section, it relates to medical trauma caused by heart or lung disease.

On the Fate Line, a cross appears when a permanent separation or divorce occurs, or when the subject is retrenched from a comfortable and secure career. Very often the Fate Line becomes stronger after these events have passed and the subject becomes wiser for the lesson.

On the Apollo Line, a cross indicates a disappointment regarding the subject's hopes and dreams, such as missed opportunities through no fault of their own. Also, people with dysfunctional family backgrounds often have a cross on the palm in the area of the Apollo Line.

Squares

Squares or boxes are formed in close proximity to an island, cross, break or weakened line as a sign of protection against the traumatic period illustrated by their existence. When the problem period is over and the time of emotional, mental or physical setback has ended, the island, cross, break, frailty and square will sometimes disappear. However, if the problem has been solved, but the impact of the trauma has left its mark, then only the square of protection will disappear.

Islands and Chains

The journey of life is often delayed or disrupted by events which are unfavorable, and illustrated warning signs appear on the palm in the form of a chain (a series of mini islands linked together) or in the case of a more serious disruption, an island.

On the Life Line, they are indicative of disruptive influences to the natural energy flow, causing periods of discomfort and weakness.

On the Head Line, they indicate problems with headaches, migraine and eyesight. If the island appears on the Mount of Saturn above that part of the Head Line, it suggests a problem with the ears.

On the Heart Line, on the "A" and "B" sections, islands and chains indicate emotional pressures which can result in health hazards. On the "C" section they indicate lung, bronchial and throat problems.

On the Fate Line, they show periods of distress caused by difficulties in career, business or partnerships.

On the Apollo Line, they suggest misguided judgment on career choice, or an unfortunate event which causes delays and disappointments in the pursuit of success.

Other Markings

Breaks on any of the major lines can be likened to the sudden break on a main highway and should be treated with the same caution as any road block. When the line continues its journey a square will often appear on or near the line indicating a recovery from mishap or danger.

Triangles will sometimes appear on the palm during times of despair, but will disappear when the problem has been solved. They are temporary nuisance signals.

Stars which appear on the Mount of Venus herald good fortune in the subject's love life; and on the Mount of Apollo, it foretells good luck with financial matters.

Grills appear on various parts of the palm when excessive energy bursts result in temporary exhaustion.

Branches and Forks are interpreted by the upward and downward direction they take and position on which they appear. Branches which shoot upwards from the line indicate improved circumstances or fortunate incidents. Branches which droop downwards represent short term disappointments. A forked line appears on a line when the energies are divided, e.g. a dual career path or divided interests.

Tasseled or Frayed Lines indicate conditions which drain the energy on the Life Line, exhausted mental energy on the Head Line, and frayed nerves, caused by overwork, on the Fate Line. On the Heart Line it indicates a hardening of the arteries or angina problems.

Rascettes of Bracelets are names given to the two or three lines which run across the length of the wrist. Many Eastern palmists used the number of "bracelets" to determine the length of the subject's life. The practice was to attribute 30 years life span to each bracelet, e.g. two full length bracelets and one half bracelet would therefore predict a lifespan of 75 years, and three full length bracelets would mean a span of 90 years. Modern palmists debate this belief. Two facts which are more easily agreed upon are that:

a) well-defined and long bracelets are indicative of a fortunate and healthy lifestyle, while short and delicate looking bracelets suggest a more difficult and less energetic lifestyle; and

b) when the bracelet nearest the palm rises in the center to form a curved appearance suggests in a female hand a gynecological problem, and in a male hand, hormonal problems.

The Family Ring is the ring which circles the base of the thumb and represents the subject's degree of dedication to the home and family. The more well defined the ring, the greater the devotion to the family. Sometimes a second family ring will appear in this area, a little higher than the main one. This occurs when the subject's life becomes involved with more than one family, e.g. an adopted family or family from a second marriage. Lines cutting across the Family Ring represent trauma caused by interference from other family members.

 THE FOLLOWING RINGS SHOULD NOT BE CONFUSED WITH THE NATURAL CREASE MARKS FOUND AT THE BASE OF EACH FINGER. THEY ARE TO BE FOUND — IF AT ALL — BELOW THOSE CREASES, USUALLY ON THE MOUNTS.

The Ring of Solomon: this ring appears on the Mount of Jupiter below the base line of the Jupiter finger and signifies the subject's desire to play a caring role in the life of others.

The Ring of Saturn: this ring is situated below the base of the Saturn finger and is considered to belong to a person who tends to cut themselves off from other people because they have poor social skills and find integrating with others difficult.

The Ring of Apollo: seldom seen, this ring is situated below the base of the Apollo finger. It contradicts the fortunate Apollo influences that are bestowed on a well-developed and well-marked Mount of Apollo. It is much like a "road block" which temporarily holds up the flow of busy traffic.

The Singles Ring: situated below the base line of the Mercury finger, this ring swoops downwards and outwards towards the Marriage Line, sometimes cutting across it. It belongs to people who are marriage shy or afraid of permanent commitment or those who repeatedly lose their partners.

The Line of Mars: this line is situated inside the Life Line on the Mount of Venus and is usually deep and well defined, suggesting a reserve supply of energy which serves as a booster to any sign of delicacy or weakness in the Life Line. It is also interesting to note that spiritual healers also bear this sign.

TIMING —
WHEN WILL I ARRIVE?

t would indeed be an advantage to know the approximate time of important events you will experience during life. You can gain greater understanding of events already experienced simply by seeing what factors contributed to them at that stage of your development.

Knowing the age you will be when major turning points are about to happen can help you prepare for life's experiences. To know when your creative or business powers are likely to be strong or weak would allow you to prepare accordingly. And to be able to take advantage of the warning signs which forecast an oncoming health hazard can forestall or lessen the impact.

Naturally, to be precise about the exact dates would take more space than a book of this size would permit. But for a rule of thumb, the end of a line represents the age of between 80 and 90, while halfway along any line represents roughly the age of 45.

On the page opposite is a diagram which gives you an approximate timing on each of the main lines of the palm.

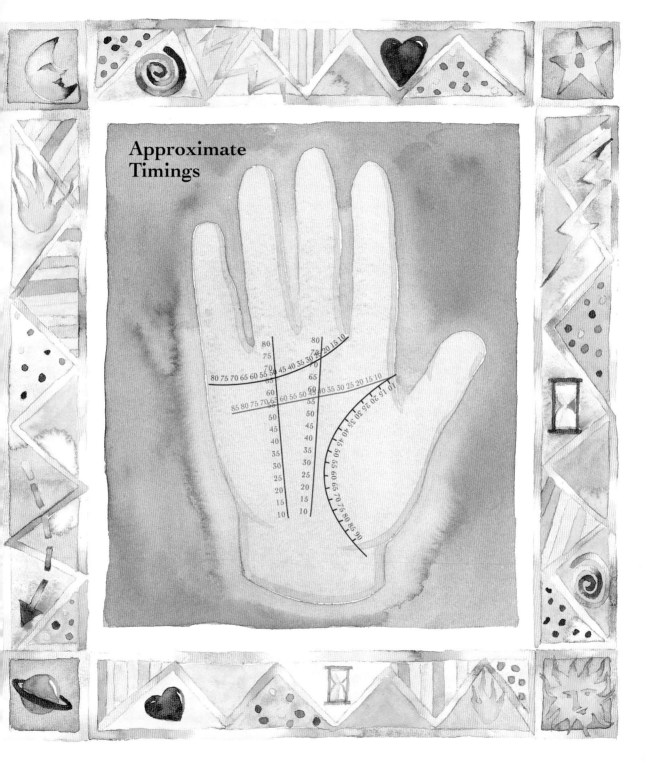

Approximate
Timings

EXAMPLE DESTINIES

Madeline

t a glance you can see that Madeline has a "full hand" (many fine lines) on a Conic-shaped hand, a long thumb, and a long Mercury finger. The finger phalanges are equally and well proportioned, all of which tells us at once that here we have an idealistic, sensitive person with creative instincts (the Conic shape). The fullness of her palm (many lines) suggests she is emotional and suffers with nerves, her highly developed imagination often causing her to expect disappointments before they arrive.

The many lines also suggest there are a lot of emotional challenges in personal relationships which can cause her to become suspicious of people's intentions and expectations. But the positive influences of the full hand will encourage her to develop her creative and artistic talents, verified by the strong lines under her Apollo finger which will eventually give her the courage and confidence to achieve her goals, especially those she hopes to achieve through her literary skills, shown by the "writers fork" on the end of her head line, the long Mercury finger which guarantees her the gift of self-expression, teaching and journalistic skills, as well as a searching mind.

This long Mercury finger with its long first and second phalanges further ensures Madeline that she is destined to fulfill her artistic and literary ambitions. The fact that this finger also has a tendency to lean towards the Apollo finger suggests she has the ability and tenacity to pursue her dreams, overcoming obstacles created by circumstance or the jealousy of rivals. The flexible and long thumb adds credence to this idea, indicating an innate staying power, enthusiasm and a logical, rational attitude.

Madeline's Life Line begins its journey high up on the palm near the Mount of Jupiter (representing ambition) and travels in a well-defined condition around a developed Mount of Venus (indicating a good quality of life with plenty of drive and applied effort) to a point

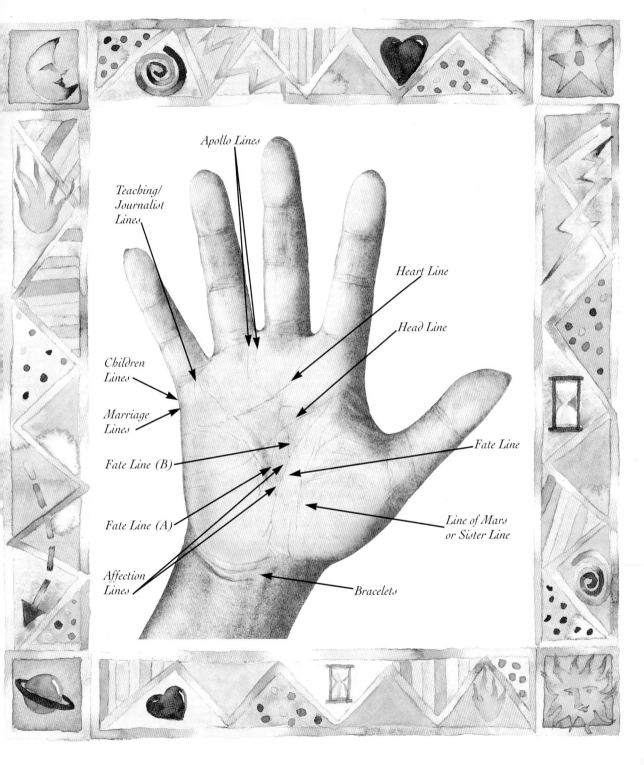

Apollo Lines

Teaching/
Journalist
Lines

Children
Lines

Marriage
Lines

Fate Line (B)

Fate Line (A)

Affection
Lines

Heart Line

Head Line

Fate Line

Line of Mars
or Sister Line

Bracelets

around the age of about 70 years where it divides into a forked appearance (showing a desire to gather experience from home and away). During her formative years (birth to 15 years) the Life Line and Head Line cross paths forming an island which indicates some trauma experienced during this time. A succession of crosses and squares sitting between the Life and Head Lines are indicative of more difficult times during her twenties and thirties, which have caused her both mental and physical exhaustion. But the squares (protection from danger) plus the appearance of a well-defined Line of Mars are her insurance that she would overcome these challenges. The Head Line on Madeline's hand is well developed and long, without the disruption of breaks or islands, curving gently down into the Mount of the Moon. This signifies a well-adjusted, level-headed personality who is also blessed with imagination, inventiveness, idealism, romance and creativity, proving that even to this point of her assessment, each line, mount, shape and marking are confirming her talented personality.

When looking at Madeline's Heart Line we must first note that Madeline has a curved Heart Line, which shows that she is an emotional person with a lot of love to give, but only to the right person for her. This is shown by her Heart Line beginning near the Mount of Jupiter, indicating that she will not settle for less than what she needs in a relationship. A note worth remembering in her case is that the combination of both a curved Head Line and Heart Line mean that Madeline will not easily forget the details of her personal relationships (the good and the bad memories). People with these two important Main Lines, both curved, can be vulnerable to partners with a jealous or dominating nature.

The Heart Line should now be divided into the 3 sections of "A" affection, "B" emotion, and "C" health. The "A" section of Madeline's Heart Line is forked at the beginning implying that she will have a practical but caring attitude to her partner. The "B" section shows a branch sloping downwards from the line, indicating a disappointing result of a relationship beginning in her early thirties which she obviously tried to maintain with all its faults since no break or island appears until much later when a dot followed by a succession of chained islands indicate the relationship ended in unhappiness due to cruelty and victimization from the partner. The "C" section is entirely made up of a feathered jagged look indicating health problems connected with the lungs.

Madeline appears to have a double Fate Line which, judging from their position and appearance — one starting on the Mount of the Moon and crossing the Head Line, joining a downwards sloping branch from the Heart Line indicating a self-motivated attitude up to that point, the other starting from a point on the Life Line, crossing the Head Line and ending on a point parallel to the other Fate Line — would strongly suggest that due to interference of an unfortunate choice of partner, the growth and expansion of an otherwise successful career would be thwarted. However, these two Fate Lines are also made up of square formations which will give protection from unscrupulous business partners. Another short line shooting upwards from the Fate Line to the Heart Line indicates that Madeline will create her own business working mainly from home.

Marriage/Children: Madeline has 2 or 3 faint lines which suggest that although they appear to be long-term relationships they will not result in a commitment of marriage. She has one only strong Marriage Line which occurs after age 40 from which she produces or "inherits" 2 children (a girl and a boy).

Summary: This gifted, creative, intelligent person will eventually gain the reward and recognition for effort and talent, and even though the first half of her lifespan is plagued by emotional trauma from family and personal relationships, she has the courage and determination to confront her problems, eventually turning the lessons learned from these experiences into advantages, therefore making the second half of her life fulfilling and rewarding.

Tim

From the Square shape of his hand, we can assume that Tim is a conventional, law-abiding citizen whose practical methodical mind will ensure him a chosen career which will provide him with the security and comfort he will inevitably seek. Typically of the Square-shaped hand, there are few lines other than the major lines appearing on the palm; also typically, these lines are well defined and easy to follow, all of which suggest that Tim is innately resourceful with a good head for business and sound financial ventures. The thumb is firmly set, further proof of his steadfastness; but this also shows a stubborn streak, which could convince him that he is right all the time.

The Life Line starts high on the palm and is joined to the Head Line until the late teens in a jagged pattern, suggesting that his early years were mostly influenced by his parents guidance, which will serve him well. However, some traumatic experience, such as the sudden separation from one or both parents, has left its mark through the crossed jagged appearance. The Life Line then continues its journey around the Mount of Venus in a fairly well-defined manner, with the exception of an island around the age of 33, signifying some dramatic incident which lasts for about 5 years. There is a break in the Life Line, which means a sudden, dramatic change of direction, between the late thirties and early forties, but whatever the drama this time, it is protected by the form of a square, enabling Tim to continue his journey in a healthy productive manner from that point onwards into old age.

The Head Line is well defined and travels across the palm into the Mount of the Moon (creativity and imagination), but being of the logical, practical type, he may prefer to trust the safety of a conventional career rather than risk all for the pursuit of a career in the creative arts. Around the age 30–33 there is a branch which shoots downwards from the Head Line and crosses the Life Line indicating some unfortunate circumstance resulting in temporary mental and physical distress. Around the mid-forties and again in the

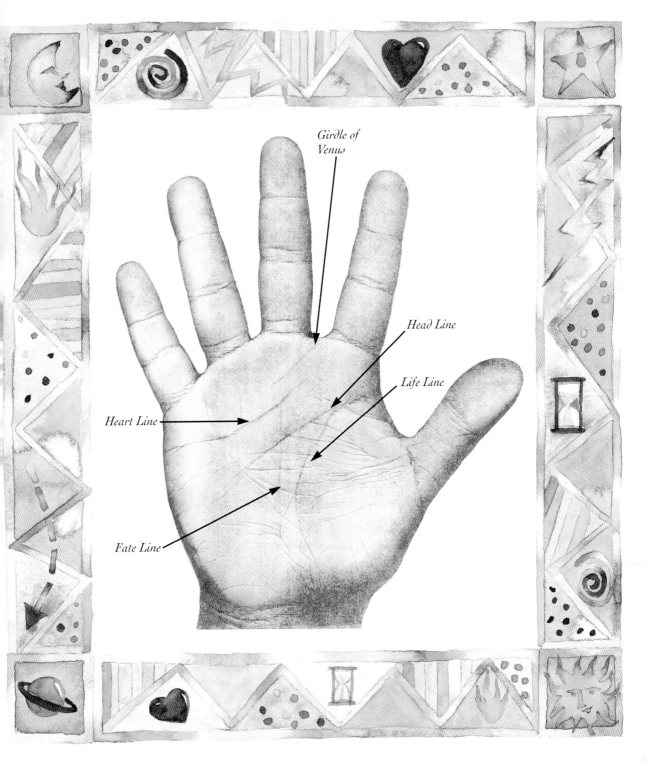

Girdle of Venus

Head Line

Life Line

Heart Line

Fate Line

mid-fifties, there is the appearance of a small dot, suggesting temporary mental exhaustion at these times, after which the Head Line continues in an undisturbed pattern into old age.

The "A" section (affection) of Tim's Heart Line which begins under the Saturn finger is the best defined of all the lines, signifying that Tim's need for emotional security is greater than all other interests. This being so, Tim has to be aware that an unscrupulous partner could easily manipulate him, causing him to become the victim of his emotional vulnerability, something which is further substantiated by the sudden dip and small gap between the "B" and "C" sections indicating a highly emotional and sensual nature. It is also at this point that a couple of small branches curving downwards appear on the line, representing emotional disappointments. The Heart Line continues after this point in a well-defined manner, suggesting that he can expect to regain control of his emotional setbacks, thus enabling him to continue his journey into later years in good health and good spirits.

The Fate Line makes its appearance beginning on the Mount of the Moon at about the age of 20 and is accompanied by a number of travel lines, some touching the Fate Line. This suggests that a union, such as one which results in a marriage commitment with someone from overseas, takes place in his mid twenties. The dot which appears at this junction suggests that for a period of time some confusion and turmoil will be experienced until they sort out in which part of the world they wish to settle. For about 5 years they will decide to settle in Tim's country, but then another dot appears followed by branches crossing the Fate Line indicating more turbulence connected with home sickness on the partner's side, by which time the added responsibility of a child occurs.

The straight well-defined Fate Line indicates a successful career path which brings material benefits. However, dots appearing again on the Fate Line at intervals, combined with dots which appear on the Head Line, suggest that Tim should make sure he combines dedication to hard work with plenty of rest and recreation otherwise he will experience depression due to an overdose of stressful responsibility.

There are no obvious Apollo Lines on Tim's hand suggesting reward and recognition for effort, but this could be because the Fate Line has already promised these benefits.

Marriage/Children: One strong Marriage Line appears on Tim's hand, confirming the Fate Line's prediction, but one or two faint lines under the Marriage Line suggest that Tim will have to be wary of extramarital relationships.

Summation: Tim has all the qualities and ability to make an interesting and successful journey of life, especially if he recognizes and establishes his priorities early. Although it is obvious he will choose a safe and secure career path to follow, he would be well advised to explore the creative side of his nature which could provide him with the necessary outlet to the burden of a stressful business career and serious family commitments.

Chances are that he will also choose a partner who is both loyal, conservative, and conscientious (all the qualities which he has himself) but the creative part of his nature could be at times attracted to a more extroverted, spontaneous personality, causing him some headaches and even at times causing him to question the commitment of his choice of marriage partner. Being a person of innate moral fiber, however, Tim is certain to think before acting.

Your personal map of life is intact
The voyage is the reward you exact
You direct the traffic — you have a voice
However and wherever you go is choice
The wisdom you gain along your travels
Reveal the truth as the plot unravels
Obstacle courses are there to surmount
Don't waste time loitering — make it all count!
Enjoy the surprise around every bend
Carving a path from beginning to end

YOUR HIGHWAY TO LIFE

Nothing is more valuable to you than the quality of your life. The time you devote to the planning and execution of your journey is precious. Nature has provided the directions it supposes you need for the experience in the form of a map of life, illustrated on the palms of your hands. When you learn to appreciate this form of assistance and put it to good use, you reap the rewards for your efforts, making the exercise both pleasant and successful. Even if or when you find yourself lost or misguided, there is always an alternative route which will return you to the right path, and hopefully you are wiser for the detour. Nothing is wasted on the journey of life if you are prepared to see the advantage of experience.

It is perfectly acceptable to "stop–revive–survive", but loitering is simply a waste of valuable time. Every aspect of life is detailed by the quality, shape, and signals shown on the lines, mounts and fingers on your hands — they are predestined, mysterious gifts for which we must be grateful. It is up to each individual to use these gifts, combine them with common sense and a joy of living, to make their lives rich and successful.

It remains only for me, therefore, to wish you God Speed and Bon Voyage in the knowledge that the information I have provided will be beneficial to the quality of your journey.

For Judy and Lizzie

First published by Lansdowne Publishing Pty Ltd, 1997
This edition published in 1998 by

Parkgate Books Ltd
Kiln House
210 New King's Road
London SW6 4NZ
Great Britain

1 3 5 7 9 8 6 4 2

British Library Cataloguing in Publication Data:
A catalogue record for this book is available from the British Library.

ISBN 1 85585 522 4

Designer: Sylvie Abecassis
Editor: Cynthia Blanche
Illustrators: Penny Lovelock, Sue Ninham

Set in Cochin, Remedy and Bauer Text Initials on QuarkXpress
Printed in Hong Kong by Mandarin Offset